Tractors On The Farm

John Allan

Hungry Tomato™

First published in 2026 by Hungry Tomato Ltd
F15, Old Bakery Studios
Blewetts Wharf
Malpas Road, Truro
Cornwall, TR1 1QH, UK

A CIP catalog record for this book is available from the British Library

ISBN 9781835696705

Manufactured in the USA

Thanks to our editor, Julie Tofflemire

Discover more at
www.hungrytomato.com

Words in **bold** can be found in the glossary

Contents

The Mighty Mechanics

We are the Mighty Mechanics. Welcome to our workshop! We work on some amazing vehicles and machines. Here are a few of the tools we use to fix them.

This torque wrench can tighten nuts and bolts so that they never get loose.

We might use a hydraulic jack to lift and move heavy tractors that need fixing.

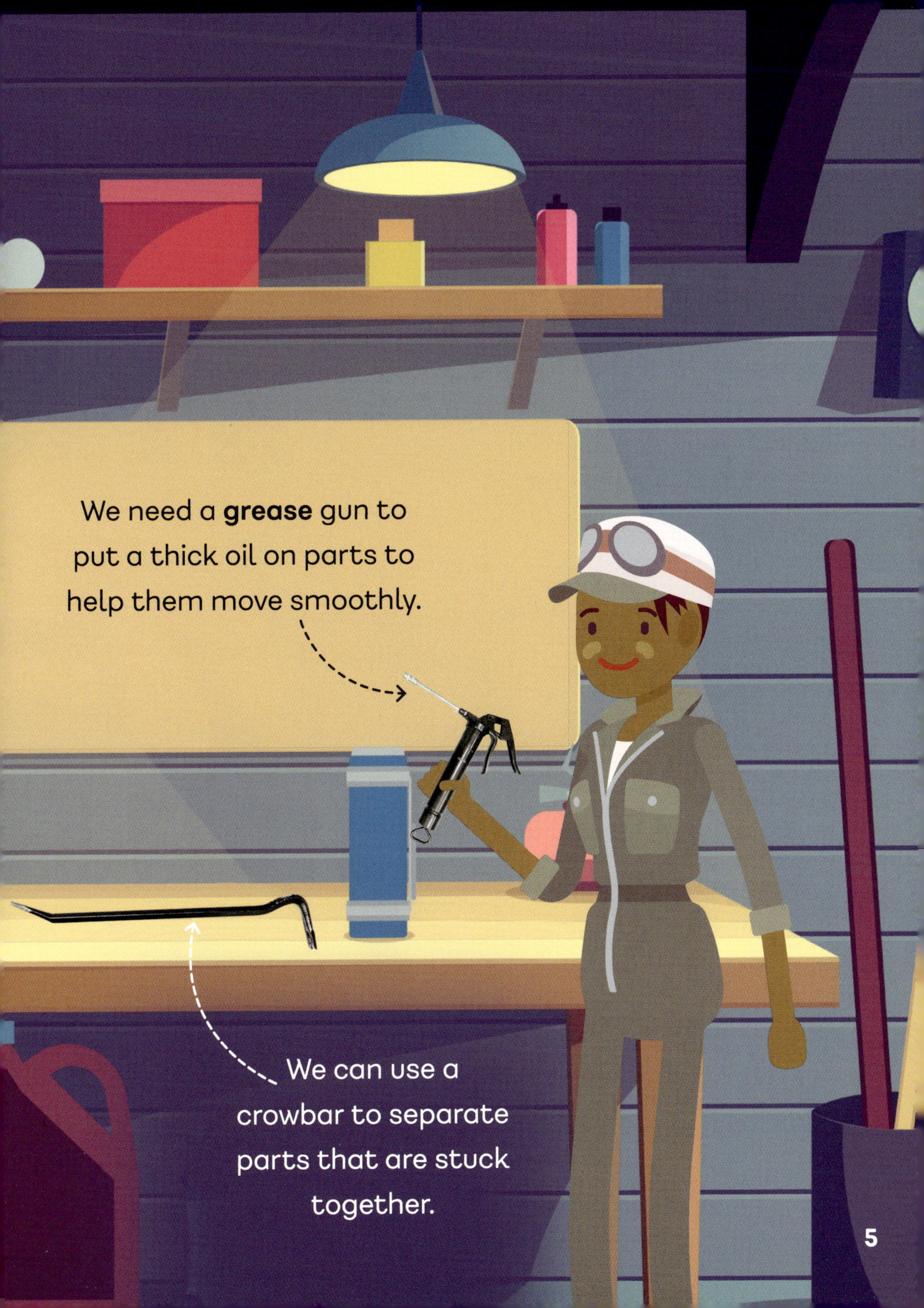

We need a **grease** gun to put a thick oil on parts to help them move smoothly.

We can use a crowbar to separate parts that are stuck together.

Utility Tractor

A utility tractor is one of the most useful vehicles on the farm! It does a lot of different jobs.

The driver sits in the cab and steers the tractor around the field.

This tractor is pulling equipment to plant seeds.

The big wheels in the back help it to move on soft ground.

Compact Tractor

For smaller jobs, a compact tractor is just the right size. It can fit into smaller spaces than a utility tractor.

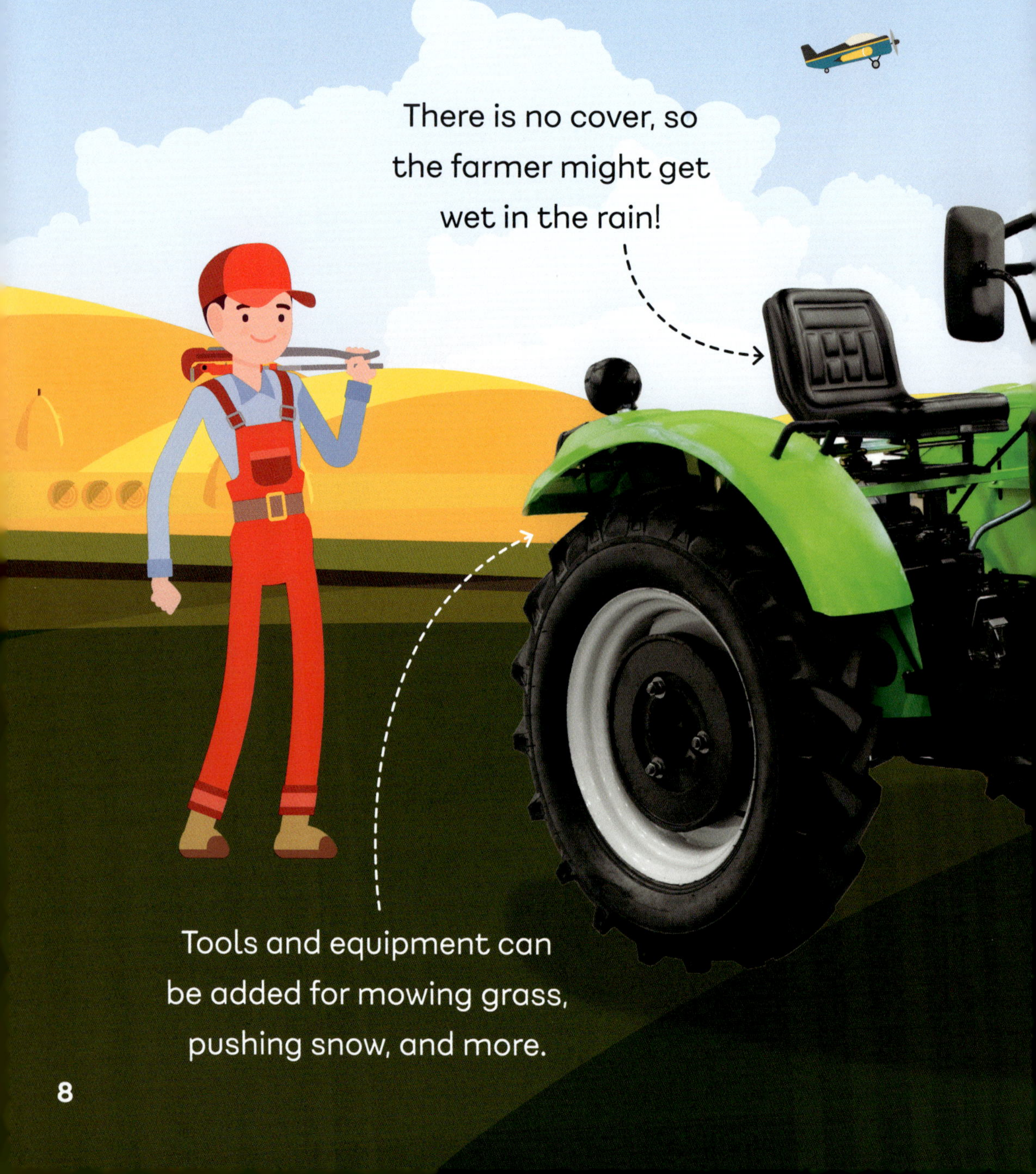

The exhaust pipe removes smoke and gases from the tractor's engine.

The patterns on the tires help them to **grip** the ground.

Crawler Tractor

This vehicle knows how to stay on track! The crawler tractor has tracks instead of wheels.

Another name for a crawler tractor is a continuous track tractor.

The tracks keep the tractor from getting stuck in the mud.

This crawler tractor is pulling equipment that breaks up the soil.

A weight at the front keeps the tractor from tipping backward.

Smart Tractor

A smart tractor is high-tech! It uses computers, a **GPS**, and sensors to do farm work. It can get a lot of work done by itself.

Some smart tractors can run for 24 hours without taking a break!

This smart tractor is pulling equipment, but no farmer is on board.

Some designs have wheels, and others have tracks.

Pickup Truck

A pickup truck has an open back, and it can drive on rough ground. It is strong enough to carry tools, hay, and even animals.

Some farms are enormous! Farmers need trucks to get around.

Trucks with an **extended** cab have room for a backseat.

The bed of the truck holds the load.

The **tailgate** in the back folds down for loading or to make room for larger items.

All-Terrain Vehicle (ATV)

An all-**terrain** vehicle – often called an ATV or quad bike – is tough! It can handle almost any kind of ground, so farmers can get around quickly.

This farmer is using an ATV to **herd** animals!

The driver doesn't need to push any pedals, so there are footrests for their feet.

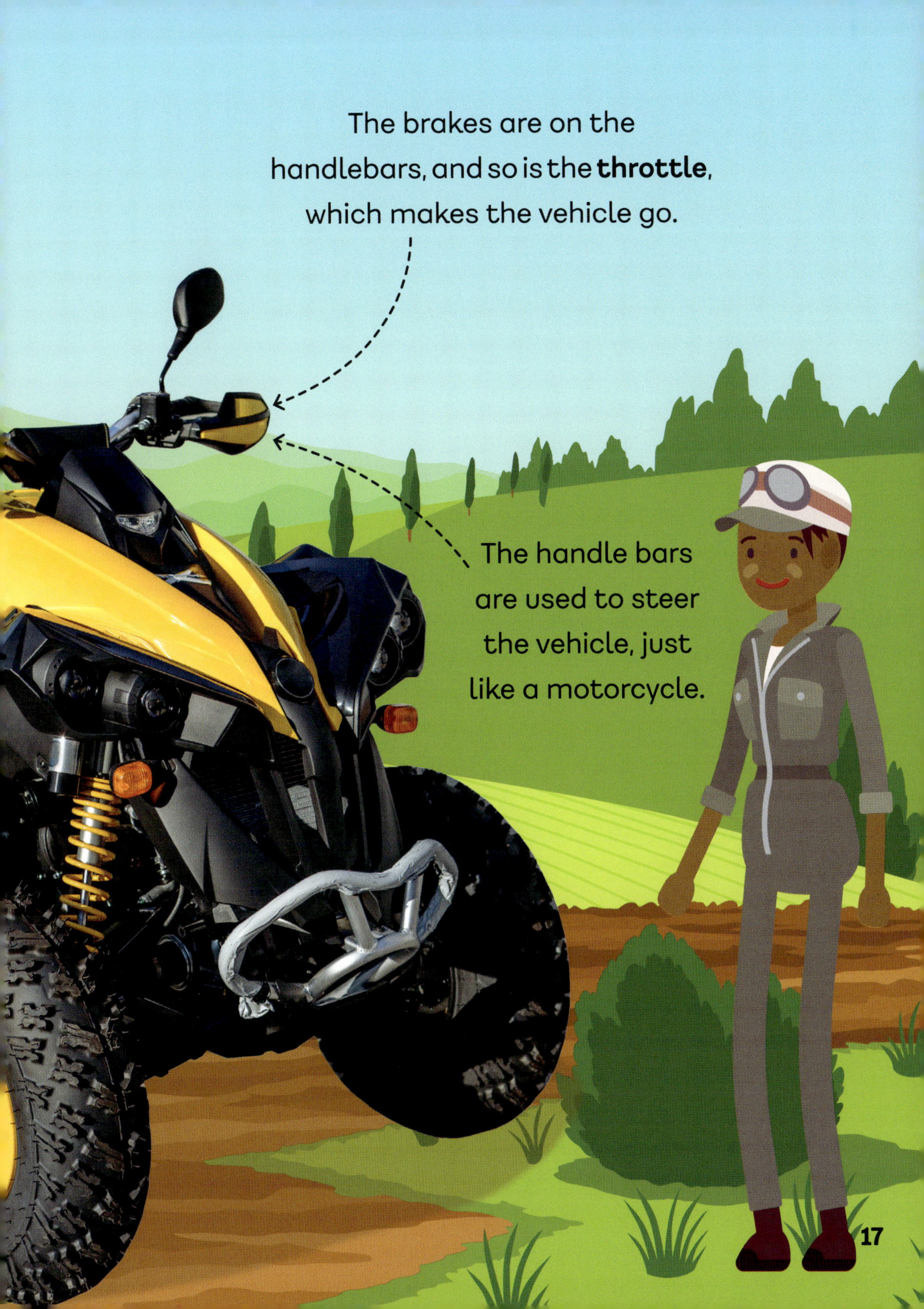

The brakes are on the handlebars, and so is the **throttle**, which makes the vehicle go.

The handle bars are used to steer the vehicle, just like a motorcycle.

Agricultural Drone

An agricultural drone is a flying robot! It can take pictures of **crops**, drop seeds, and spray fields.

Drones usually have four, six, or eight **propellers**.

An agricultural drone is usually about the size of a ride-on lawnmower.

Drones can work in the field even if the farmer is far away.

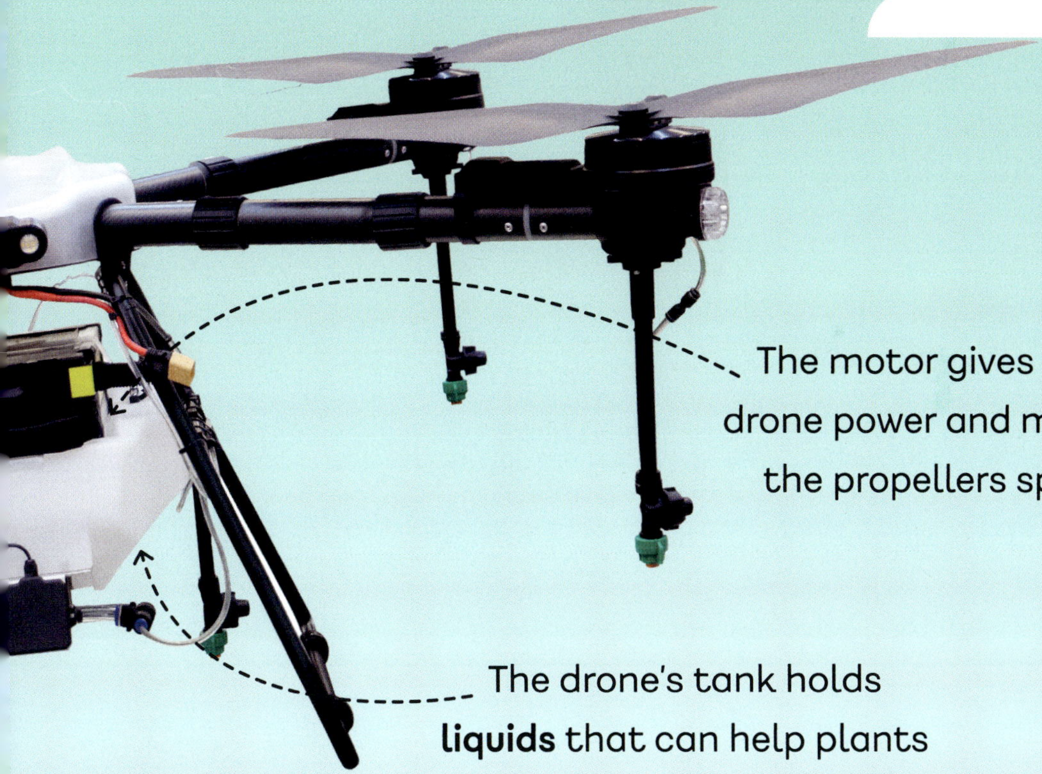

The motor gives the drone power and makes the propellers spin.

The drone's tank holds **liquids** that can help plants grow or stop weeds.

Skid Steer Loader

A skid steer loader lifts, moves, and digs things! It is great for jobs with hay, **grain**, dirt, or food for the animals.

This skid steer loader is pushing harvested rice into a pile.

The bucket can scoop up heavy loads again and again.

Skid steer loaders can spin in a circle, so they are good for working in small spaces.

The boom arms move up and down to lift the bucket.

Weather Station

Farmers need to know a lot about the weather so they can take care of their crops. A weather station gives them the information they need.

Spinning cups move when the wind blows, measuring the wind speed.

A special container collects the rain to see how much has fallen.

Weather information tells farmers when to plant and water their crops.

This weather station is reporting information back to the farmer.

The station uses solar power, so it doesn't need an electricity line.

Glossary

Crops – plants grown for food.

Extended – something that has been made longer.

Grain – small, hard seeds from food plants such as rice or wheat.

Grease – a thick, oily material often used to make machines run more smoothly.

Grip – to hold tightly.

GPS – Global Positioning System, a system that uses satellites in space to find the exact location of something.

Herd – to make animals come together in a group.

Liquids – substances that flow freely such as water, juice, or milk.

Propellers – long, flat parts on a plane that turn to make the plane move forward.

Sensors – a machine part that notices changes around it in things like light, temperature, or movement, and sends this information to other devices.

Tailgate – a door at the back of a vehicle that opens downward.

Terrain – ground or land.

Throttle – the part that controls how much fuel goes into an engine and makes the vehicle go.

Picture Credits
(abbreviations: t = top; b = bottom; m = middle; l = left; r = right; bg = background)

Andrew Rybalko (characters throughout); Cherdchai101 20mr; Droidworker 8-9bg, Dvande 7tr; Gan chaonan 19tr; Gargantiopa 20-21m;Hrach Hovhannisyan 14-15m; Ian Dewar Photography 11tr; Kwangmoozaa 18-19m; Lukas Puchrik 23bm; Madpixel 6-7bg, 22-23bg; Malika Keehl 18-19bg; Marcelo F Junior 14ml; Matveev Aleksandr 8-9m; Photobac 6-7m; Scharfsinn 12-13m, 13tr; Snapshoot freddy 22-23m; Sotisare 10-11bg; Stefan11 10-11m; The8monkey 16-17bg; Valentin Vlakov 16-17m; Vector pocket 4-5bg; Warren Design 9mr.